KALIYA
Serpent King

KALIYA
Serpent King

Joshua M. Greene
ILLUSTRATIONS BY Patrick Wire

INSIGHT KIDS
A MANDALA BOOK

San Rafael, California

Once there was an island of serpents. Their king, Kaliya, was a many-headed serpent, the largest and strongest of them all. He decorated his heads with royal jewels. He breathed hot fire from his mouths and poisonous fumes from his nostrils. Kaliya was dangerous, powerful, and very proud.

One creature was stronger than Kaliya: a giant eagle named Garuda. Like all eagles, Garuda had a taste for serpents. To avoid being eaten, the snakes on the island cooked pots of food and placed them on a hill. Garuda ate the food and left the serpents alone.

One day Kaliya slithered up the hill. "Hisss! Why should that bird get all this delicious food?" he said, and he stuck his tongues into the pots and began eating. Garuda learned that Kaliya was stealing his food and rushed to the hill. Kaliya slithered quickly away.

Garuda swatted Kaliya with his giant wings. Kaliya fought with his powerful hoods. Garuda was stronger. He grabbed Kaliya in his talons. "For stealing my food," he said, "you must leave this island forever."

Kaliya was afraid of the mighty eagle. He gathered his wives and children, and off they went. They swam day and night until they came to a river called the Yamuna. In the river Kaliya found a pool large enough for his family, and there they stayed.

Kaliya was no longer king, but he still enjoyed breathing out fire and fumes. Trees withered. Grass shriveled. The water smelled. Fish closed their eyes and floated to the surface. A sickly mist rose up from the river. Birds flying through the mist fell lifeless to the ground. The beautiful Yamuna and the surrounding land were a place of doom.

Near the river sat the village of Vrindavan, where young Krishna lived. Not long after Kaliya's arrival, Krishna was playing with his cowherd friends. They were tending the calves, singing songs, and inventing games in the shade of flowering trees.

The cowherd boys grew thirsty and ran to the river. As soon as their lips touched the water, they fell lifeless to the ground, for Kaliya's poison acted quickly.

Krishna found his friends and looked at each one with love. Those loving glances brought his friends back to life. Then Krishna saw the withered trees, shriveled grass, and polluted water. "Something must be done," he thought. Krishna climbed to the top of a big tree, tightened his belt, flapped his arms, and dove into the water.

Splash!

"Hisss! Someone has invaded our home,"
Kaliya said. Out he swam, looking for a fight.

Kaliya spotted Krishna. "He is nothing but a little boy," he thought and grabbed Krishna with his mighty coils, raising him high in the air. Krishna played along, pretending to be an ordinary boy.

Nature herself feared for Krishna's safety. Meteors fell from the sky, and an earthquake shook the ground beneath Vrindavan. "Where is our child?" cried Krishna's mother and father. "He must be in danger." They gathered the villagers and set out to find him.

They followed Krishna's footprints and came to the Yamuna River. The cowherd boys pointed to Krishna trapped in Kaliya's coils, and everyone cried out in fear. Krishna's mother tried to run into the river, for a mother's love knows no limits. Friends held her back.

When Krishna saw his frightened parents and friends, he stopped pretending to be an ordinary boy. He flexed his arms, puffed up his chest, and broke Kaliya's grasp.

"Hisss!" Kaliya said.

The giant serpent blew fire from his mouths and fumes from his nostrils. He snapped at Krishna, but Krishna jumped away. He danced and kicked and stamped a footprint onto each of Kaliya's many hoods.

Kaliya grew weak from the blows of Krishna's feet. He struggled to breathe. The giant serpent fainted, and his coils went slack.

Kaliya's wives swam up to Krishna with folded hands. "In his last life," they said, "our husband must have been very cruel. Why else would he be such a nasty serpent in this life? By dancing on his hoods, you have beaten the poison out of him. And that is good. But if you continue, he will not survive. Our children will be fatherless, and we will be widows. Kaliya polluted the Yamuna out of ignorance. Won't you please forgive him?"

At that moment, Kaliya awoke and bowed to Krishna. "I was born angry and proud," he said. "You have forced me to change my ways. Forgive me for polluting your river and hurting your friends. Tell me how to show you I am sorry."

"Dear Kaliya," Krishna said—for everyone is dear to Krishna—"it is my duty to protect the river. The river provides drinking water. The river nourishes the trees and fields. The river is home to so many creatures. I had to stop you from polluting the Yamuna. Please do not be unhappy with me.

"You came here out of fear of Garuda, but he will not bother you anymore. He will see my footprints on your hoods and leave you alone.

"Still, I must ask you to leave so that the Yamuna will never be poisoned again. May the rivers run pure and clear, and may people and animals live in peace."

Kaliya bowed again to Krishna. Then he and his wives and children swam out to sea, where they soon found a new home and lived happily.

Krishna waded out of the Yamuna.
The villagers rushed forward, hugging
him and calling his name, "Krishna! Krishna!"
His mother and father shed tears of joy.

Trees and flowers once again blossomed along the river. Grass grew sweet and green once more. The water turned remarkably clear and blue. Fish swam and birds flew. Vrindavan returned to life, setting the scene for more of Krishna's adventures . . .

Adventures so extraordinary, they are worth telling another time, in another book.

~ The End ~

A Note to Parents and Teachers

KALIYA is a retelling of an ancient Vedic tale that has been passed on for centuries in the oral tradition from parents to children—a tradition steeped in deep respect for nature, and one that recognizes divinity in all things. Many wisdom tales from India feature child Krishna and friends overcoming a monster or tyrant who symbolizes a threat to the natural environment. Taken from the Sanskrit Bhagavata Purana, these tales describe Krishna as the Supreme Being playing human to protect the world and instruct humanity. In this story, Kaliya symbolizes those who pollute our sacred rivers. Today, the same Yamuna River is facing extreme challenges from many such polluters. Whether one views Krishna as human or divine, his role in protecting the natural world has endeared him to children and adults alike for thousands of years.

INSIGHT KIDS
A MANDALA BOOK

PO Box 3088
San Rafael, CA 94912
www.insighteditions.com

Library of Congress Cataloging-in-Publication Data available.

ISBN: 978-1-60887-148-3

Design by Dagmar Trojanek

ROOTS of PEACE   REPLANTED PAPER

Insight Editions, in association with Roots of Peace, will plant two trees
for each tree used in the manufacturing of this book. Roots of Peace is
an internationally renowned humanitarian organization dedicated to
eradicating land mines worldwide and converting war-torn lands into
productive farms and wildlife habitats. Together, we will plant two
million fruit and nut trees in Afghanistan and provide farmers there
with the skills and support necessary for sustainable land use.

Manufactured in China by Insight Editions

10 9 8 7 6 5 4 3 2 1